the
BRIDE'S RITUAL GUIDE

the BRIDE'S RITUAL GUIDE

LOOK INSIDE TO FIND YOURSELF

CORNELIA POWELL

something for all women who love matters of the heart

Library of Congress Control Number: 2009904025
ISBN: 1-4392-5491-5
ISBN: 978-1-4392-5491-2

PRINTED IN THE UNITED STATES OF AMERICA

What People Are Saying About Cornelia Powell and *The Bride's Ritual Guide: Look Inside to Find Yourself*

"**Cornelia** is a wise voice on what weddings are meant to be: stylish *and* sacred, fun *and* deeply meaningful. I think every bride needs her message: that every choice you make—from your dress to your vows—is an opportunity to your authentic self."

—Danielle LaPorte, Creator of WhiteHotTruth.com;
lead author of *Style Statement: Live By Your Own Design*

"**Cornelia Powell** has captured the true spirit of weddings in her writings and in her advice to brides. She mixes to perfection tradition and style."

—Phyllis Hoffman, Publisher, *Victoria* magazine

"**Cornelia Powell** is the spokesperson for brides who want elegance with intimacy, style with grace. When you read her words, they seem to fall off the pages like she's speaking right to your heart. Her words flow in a way that you want to tie a ribbon around them and hold them close to you."

—Jeanne Dudley Smith, Designer, Jeanne's Fantasia

"**Cornelia Powell** brings wisdom and joy back to the wedding experience. Her book is a must read for any bride who seeks a magical journey to the altar."

—Rev. Laurie Sue Brockway, Interfaith minister;
author of *Wedding Goddess: A Divine Guide to Transforming Wedding Stress into Wedding Bliss*

"I absolutely love **Cornelia's** take on the intuitive and very feminine aspects of the wedding event for women…

—Anik Keuller, Floral designer

"There is something magical about trying on the 'perfect' wedding gown that somehow makes the whole wedding fall into place and come alive. It's difficult to explain this incredible relationship that a bride has with her gown and **Cornelia Powell** is truly the only one who is able to eloquently and succinctly articulate this special bond that joins not only the bride with her dress, but with all the other bridal rituals that make a wedding unforgettable …."

—Lara Meiland-Shaw, Couture bridal designer,
Lara Hélène Bridal Atelier

"…our meeting with **Cornelia** made such a difference, not just how it changed wedding planning activities, but also in our relationship. My daughter, the bride-to-be, created more ease around her deadlines, became comfortable with simplicity, and incorporated all her friends into the wedding event—something good for the budget as well as a sense of sisterhood. For me, the experience with Cornelia's wise counsel was a graceful acknowledgment to me that this is my daughter's time and it was ok to step back. It was a gentle ritual of generations changing places in a private coming of age ceremony to a young woman planning her wedding and a mother letting go. Cornelia's message was a gift of relaxation to the bride—and to her mother!"

—Maureen Nolan, ACC, "Your Attention Coach"

This book is dedicated to future brides of all ages and to couples of all persuasions and to their intimate rites-of-passage ahead; to women who are moving through "grown-up" rites-of-passage of all types; and to young girls who are going through some of the more tender passages. This is also dedicated to all the women and men who support us in opening our hearts and having the courage to live in the magic that pours forth.

CONTENTS

PREFACE
W hy Ritual? *I Will Tell Thee a Supreme Mystery* xv

ABOUT THE AUTHOR xix

INTRODUCTION
Finding the Heart of Your Bridal Rite-of-Passage xxi

PART I. BECOMING RITUAL WISE

1. Bridal Rhyme Lore and History
   Tokens of Abundance 3

2. Twist on a Bridal Favorite
   Deepening Your Bridal Experience 11

3. How to Use the *RitualWise* Bridal Notes
   (plus a "Meditative Bridal Ritual" Option) 15

⟋COLLECTION OF *RITUALWISE* BRIDAL NOTES

   Section One: *Something Old* 23

   Section Two: *Something New* 37

   Section Three: *Something Borrowed* 51

   Section Four: *Something Blue* 65

   Section Five: *A Sixpence for Your Shoe* 79

PART II. WOMEN'S WISDOM

1. You and the Women Around You..95

2. How to Use Your *Wisdom Journal*..99

⟋ *WISDOM JOURNAL* PAGES 101

POSTSCRIPT
Woman-to-Woman
"Something Borrowed" Ritual Exchange:
Share Your Bridal Experience...137

PRODUCTS AND RESOURCES
Ideas from the *RitualWise* Bridal Notes..............................139

ACKNOWLEDGMENTS...143

PHOTOGRAPH CREDITS 145

BIBLIOGRAPHY 147

INDEX 151

PREFACE

Why Ritual?

I Will Tell Thee a Supreme Mystery[1]

What's a wedding without some sort of ceremony, and what's a ceremony without reenacting a ritual or two, and what's a ritual without a bit of mystery? The rituals of wedding ceremonies—such as exchanging rings, repeating vows, or even dressing in special clothes—are intended as outer expressions of our inner transformation. Rituals act as guideposts on this rather mysterious transformational journey called being a bride, this womanly rite-of-passage.

The essence of rituals comes out of the ancient past from early cultures where one's life was deeply connected to nature and the spirit world. They may come from the past, but rituals are alive and creative, full of energy as vibrant as what you're willing to put into them. The magic is not the ritual itself, but where it takes you. And that journey is within.

"The origin of rituals overlaps our own origin to the beginning of the human story—to the core of what it is to be human,"[2] scholars declare. When we participate in these ancient rituals today, we tap into the essence of our own origin. Even in our consumer-driven, frenetic

1   The Bhagavad Gita
2   The Etruscans, Fernbank Science Center exhibition, Atlanta, GA, January, 2004

technological world, rituals—when used consciously—are a way to stay linked to our true inner nature.

Defined as "a set of prescribed behaviors,"[3] rituals are designed to guide you through times that may otherwise be stressful (like a wedding ceremony), allowing you to express the ideas and feelings of your heart when your busy, "over thinking" mind may be a bit befuddled. I tell brides to trust the process. Ritual can bring order out of chaos and help ease the anxieties of the day, creating a space of intimacy and an open expression of love.

As historian Carol McD. Wallace states in her book *All Dressed in White*, "Ritual time is different from ordinary time."[4] Once the ritual process begins, something larger than yourself takes over; you relax into an inner rhythm that moves you into a meditative space. From this quiet, more settled place, you are guided through all the nuances of the rite-of-passage of growth and emergence—and a bit of mystery.

Engaging in ceremonial rituals for your wedding provides an opening into your interior life, an awareness that keeps growing after the wedding with a bit of practice. Notice what happens when you create a ritual out of an everyday task—like making a cup of tea, washing the dishes, wrapping a birthday present. You bring a deeper awareness and thoughtfulness to the process that becomes enlivening. You notice things, your world gets bigger, your heart expands, life becomes sweeter. You may even hear a soft voice saying, "*I will tell thee a supreme mystery.*"

[Reprinted from *Weddings of Grace: The Bride You Want to Be, The Woman You Become* Online Magazine; Autumn 2006. www.WeddingsOfGrace.com]

PHOTOGRAPH BY JULIE MIKOS

---

3   Carol McD. Wallace, *All Dressed in White*, (New York: Penguin Books, 2004), 3.
4   Wallace, 4.

ABOUT THE AUTHOR

*W*orking with thousands of brides for over twenty-five years, and then writing about the experiences, Cornelia Powell became known as "the bride's sage" and "a wedding folklorist." She first made headlines in the world of weddings with her innovative bridal art-to-wear boutique in Atlanta in the 1980s and '90s. The nationally recognized store provided an elegant and unique alternative to the traditional bridal shops of the time and became a haven for "grown-up" brides of all ages.

While others tend to focus on the trappings of the wedding, Cornelia focuses on the intimacy of a bride's rite-of-passage. She brings this awareness and a soothing voice to a worldwide audience in her online magazine, *Weddings of Grace* (www.WeddingsOfGrace.com). Cornelia's latest blog, "Letters to a Bride," joins *Weddings of Grace* as another heart-centered guide and together they create a "modern mythology" for today's bride.

In her books, articles, blogs and as a sought after public speaker, Cornelia uses the language of ritual and relationship, costume and folklore, stillness and self-discovery to speak to the hearts of all women. She shares ways to bring more ease, pleasure, and reassurance into a woman's life, not only as a bride, but also through her many ongoing rites-of-passage.

INTRODUCTION

Finding the Heart of Your Bridal Rite-of-Passage

ome go on an exploration with me! It's a journey that taps into the ancient wisdom and magic of the past where you uncover some of the mysteries of your bridal rite-of-passage. As you take a few calming deep breaths, the journey gently spirals inward—like a long soothing sigh—into a quiet, still space where you feel more peaceful and present. Here you are invited to *"look inside to find yourself"*...and once there, with eyes open wide, you get a glimpse of your heart's desire.

Even if you are a grown-up bride—a woman of experience, direction, and clarity—your time as a bride is a time of self-discovery. Even if you're not a bride-to-be, or if you were a bride long ago or only last year, there is something here for you. There is something for you on this journey no matter your culture or traditions. Indeed, this book offers an exploration into the heart of being a woman and encouragement to celebrate all you encounter there!

Inside these pages, you'll find the *RitualWise* **Bridal Notes**. A collection of musings inspired by the intimacy evoked between generations of women by the familiar bridal rhyme "*Something old, something new, something borrowed, something blue, and a sixpence for your shoe.*" These stories and observations take you closer to your inner spirit, opening a new awareness to "the bride you want to be and the woman you become."

When reading the *RitualWise* **Bridal Notes**—whether the folkloric rhyme is part of your heritage or not—you get to explore the history of bridal legends, discover the depth of your own heart, and deepen the connection of your relationship. And like love, there's a bit of magic that speaks all languages.

You'll also find a "something borrowed" back-of-the-book surprise. A *Wisdom Journal* that connects you to a lineage of women's voices with their words of inspiration—a bit of "borrowed" wisdom just for you. Here a space is provided to jot down insights noticed during your rite-of-passage as a bride and newlywed, creating a "heart diary" of your experience.

Along this journey, as you continue to take deep relaxing breaths and listen for the quiet within, you just may hear the voice you've been waiting for. A voice, or perhaps it's more like a feeling, guiding you into the loving sureness of your heart center. Here you find the intimacy of the stillness within…you find yourself.

PHOTOGRAPH BY JULIE MIKOS

PART I

*B*ECOMING RITUAL WISE

PHOTOGRAPH BY PRISCILLA WANNAMAKER

1. BRIDAL RHYME LORE AND HISTORY

Tokens of Abundance

My customers and audiences are always curious about the origin of wedding rituals—customs so familiar that we seldom give them a second thought during wedding festivities: tossing the garter, carrying a bouquet, exchanging rings, cutting the cake. We have accepted these traditions from the past into our modern celebrations, yet a bit of mystery remains. Most wedding rituals used today are a custom "rooted in the potent mix of tradition and superstition," states Barbara Tober, former editor in chief of *Bride's* magazine, in her classic book *The Bride: A Celebration.*

Given the hazy origin of most wedding customs, tracing them becomes a bit of a puzzle. Cultures around the world participated in wedding ceremonies in ways unique to their tribe or region or religion. These rituals and customs then took a meandering path through the centuries, being adapted and altered by new generations. To borrow a phrase from Carol McD. Wallace in her book *All Dressed in White*, wedding traditions have "complicated roots."

Mystery & Superstition

Take the rhyme, *"Something old, something new, something borrowed, something blue, and a sixpence for your shoe"*—the familiar little verse that became a beloved personal ritual for generations of brides. The rhyme itself may not be that old, but the customs it describes have been around for centuries. In cultures worldwide and for as long as we know, there was some sort of superstitious custom for brides to tuck a little token of abundance (pieces of bread, a lump of sugar, coins, a bit of ribbon, a silver charm) into their purse, glove, or shoe or sew the items into the hem of their dress. This was all done in the desire to call forth good luck, great fortune—including lots of healthy children—or some magical promise of love forever!

Shoe historian Cameron Kippen declares that throughout ancient times "it was widely accounted wearing something borrowed was lucky. The *something borrowed* varied to *something golden* or *something stolen*. A common belief was the bride would enjoy the same luck as the previous owner if the shoes of another happy bride were worn." And the good luck superstitions extended to the groom by wearing old boots loaned to him for his wedding.

The historian also reminds us that "a long standing bridal superstition stated no harm could befall a bride wearing blue." Through the ages, wide-ranging references to the color blue surround it with compelling and even divine properties. The color is often associated with the Virgin Mary and is cited in Geoffrey Chaucer's fourteenth century "The Squire's Tale" from *The Canterbury Tales* as a symbol of truth and faithfulness.

A Rhyme's Tale

With such rich folkloric history, it stands to reason that somewhere along the way, some sentimental poet put it all together in a romantic rhyme. A rhyme composed, perchance, as a gift to an adored bride, her name unknown to us now, but like brides before and since, their images became an icon of womanhood.

In their beautiful book, *Wedding Ceremonies: Ethnic Symbols, Costume and Rituals*, authors Tiziana and Gianni Baldizzone write: "Wedding rites and traditions often have the goal of ensuring good fortune for the happy couple and of protecting them from harm. The tradition of wearing 'something old, something new, something borrowed, something blue,' for instance, derives from an old Italian saying originally designed to bring the bride good luck and make the birth of a male heir more likely."

Most of the sources I read about the rhyme's origin declare it's British, with the sixpence addition specific to Scotland. However, as with most rituals, it's more likely there is a shared origin—a little this from that culture, a little that from this era—more of those "complicated roots."

Perhaps *all* that we consider as "history" has a bit of invention. Traditions are not necessarily based on facts, just a swirl of beliefs, interpretations and folklore that have congealed over time into a "tradition." So sifting through lots of conflicting information (and some of that "invented history"), I read that the now famous *"something old, something new"* bridal rhyme first appeared in print in nineteenth-century England, "ascribed to some Lancashire friends" according to Cameron Kippen's research.

Victorian Influence

Whether 'tis true or not, Victorians loved sentiment, ornamentation, and proper etiquette; so it's certainly plausible that someone from that era created the rhyme. It suits the Victorian sensibility to "clean up" all of those random, superstitious, and sometimes crude ancient practices and neatly package them into a charming little poetic directive for the bride.

Whatever the origin of the rhyming verse, the Victorians clearly popularized its use until it became ingrained into the European-American culture. And now versions of the rhyme continue to be a treasured part of many universal wedding traditions. However, there's more to uncover.

English author and historian, Ann Monsarrat, in her 1973 book *And the Bride Wore…The Story of the White Wedding*, gives us a well-researched and fascinating history of wedding customs. I discovered the out-of-print book in 1988 at the Museum of Costume's library of the Fashion Research Centre in Bath, England. Thrilled to later find a copy to include in my own research library through a used bookstore in Atlanta (this long before the phenomenon and ease of searching the Internet), I continue to count on its wealth of information. This is what Ann writes about the *"something old"* rhyme:

> *The wedding superstition with the greatest following of all in the 20th century is that a bride should wear:*
>
> *Something old, something new,*
>
> *Something borrowed, and something blue*
>
> *And, possibly, a 'silver sixpence in her shoe'. This is usually described as 'ancient' and 'traditional', its origins 'lost in the mists of time', but John Cordy Jeaffreson, who wrote on every conceivable and inconceivable aspect of the wedding in 1872 did not mention it, nor did that other mine of marriage lore, Dr. Brand in his Popular Antiquities. [circa 1777] (Neither of them mention tossing the bouquet, either—another wedding custom which is younger than it looks.) Most 20th century books of quotations and phrases and fables also ignore 'Something old, something new', but a sprightly friend in her mid-eighties tells me: 'My Mother was married in 1889, and she used it at her wedding. When I married first in 1922, I heard it for the first time from her, as she pinned a "blue" bow on to the bottom of my youthful corselette just before I went to Church! The "old" was covered by my great-great-grandmother's wedding veil, the "new" by other garments!'*

Ann says that she also knew of a 1914 bride in America who followed the custom but without the sixpence in the shoe. The author reports however that "the coin was firmly established as part of the magic" by 1966 when the second daughter of President and Mrs. Lyndon B. Johnson, Luci Baines Johnson, married. In fact, she was sent several sixpence coins from "well-wishers across the States." (For a bit of American history, Ann tells us that other good-luck tokens Luci received were "a 58-year-old lace handkerchief made by her great-grandmother, a rosary given to her sister by Pope John XXIII, and a gold locket tied with blue ribbon. She also had her name and date of the wedding day embroidered in blue on the hem of her wedding gown, which could have served for the 'something blue', too.")

Participating in a Legend

Perhaps we can't know the exact history or age of the now legendary rhyme, but the mystery may be part of the appeal and why modern brides continue to follow its "instruction" for their wedding. I believe that part of its longevity is not because it's simple and quaint and easy to follow, but because it calls forth our feminine nature and becomes a gesture of gratitude and inclusion at times when words are not always easily available. As a bride, whether you borrow your grandmother's handkerchief; carry your aunt's beaded handbag; wear a friend's heirloom veil; or pin a blue silk ribbon to your corset, you have put something magical into motion. This little bridal rhyme, in its intimate whimsy, links you to a long lineage of brides and to the beauty and mystery of womanhood.

Yes, the *"something old, something new"* rhyme inspires things for a bride to wear or carry on her wedding day. But the main point of participating in rituals is how they take you closer to the true expression of your heart, opening the way to make a lasting (and possibly healing) connection with family members and friends. And when you participate in that spirit, rituals can invoke all you hold dear because they include a tender part of *you*!

Glittering Confection

So with wedding customs and stories morphing over time to suit the ideals of a particular culture, no wonder they are infused with a kind of fairy tale quality. Folklore from our heritage that now reveals itself rather mysteriously…even veiled in a bit of magic. (And who knows? The ancient recognition of the "law of attraction" just may have been the background of these superstitions. By positively aligning your energy and thoughts to their "good luck" intentions, then the token's abundant and happy blessings would truly be yours!)

Nevertheless, wedding traditions continue whether their origins are from ancient superstitions or inspired sacred text or the desire for something meaningful and full of grace. Each generation chooses different ingredients—some old, some new—and stirs up their own celebratory version of the marriage ceremony. And it comes out like the proverbial wedding cake: beautifully decorated, full of sweet things, and topped by a bride and groom! Then, as Ann Monsarrat exclaims, "the whole glittering confection" inspires the next generation to discover something *old* that seems *new* again.

As you are planning your wedding, have fun with the delightful "wondering" quality of bridal folklore. Its mysterious and slightly out of reach qualities give your rite-of-passage a depth, vitality, and lightheartedness that reaches deep into your heart and soul. Enjoy the journey!

2. TWIST ON A BRIDAL FAVORITE

Deepening Your Bridal Experience

As many years as the *"something old, something new, something borrowed, something blue, and a sixpence for your shoe"* bridal rhyme has been touching women's lives, there are that many interpretations of its meaning, each offering suggestions for a fulfilling and happy life. For this book, and as a gift to the modern bride, I've interwoven intuitive twists and insights for a more introspective interpretation. Taking the rhyme's simplicity, I wrapped it with the intimacy of a woman's language as a way to move you deep into the heart of your bridal rite-of-passage.

Something old—"Something of remembrance and femininity": To connect your life with a legacy of women who have traveled along this path

Something new—"Something of possibility and self-discovery": The aliveness of being truly present to love in each moment

Something borrowed—"Something precious and full of grace": Sharing beauty and insights; connecting the present with the wisdom of the past and the possibility of the future

Something blue—"Something intimate and magical":
A sweet and tender connection to something divine; a reminder of
the depth and eloquence of love without conditions

A sixpence for your shoe—"Something rich with relationship":
A grounded life full of gratitude and true abundance

With the spirit of these new interpretations in the background, I
then created the collection of *RitualWise* **Bridal Notes**. My intention
for the **Notes** is that they will feed your feminine spirit, infuse your rite-
of-passage with something vibrant and meaningful, as well as reveal a
few secrets for being a more beautiful bride. And as a perk while you're
reading them, you just may find your inner goddess!

3. HOW TO USE THE
RitualWise Bridal Notes

he pleasure and engaging quality of the ***RitualWise* Bridal Notes** work whether you just read them in order one by one; or use a bit of your bridal *sixth sense* and intuitively select random ones to read at your leisure—perhaps as a soothing message for the day; or select one **Note** from each of the five sections to read together as a kind of "bridal reverie," using the following guide to create your own personal "meditative bridal ritual."

Whatever you choose, have fun with the process and use the ***Wisdom Journal*** that comes after the collection of ***RitualWise* Bridal Notes** to record your thoughts and create a wedding keepsake all at the same time! As you explore, just use your heart for a roadmap as you *"look inside to find yourself."*

(What's next? You can now read and play with the "meditative bridal ritual" suggestions that follow or go directly to the ***RitualWise* Bridal Note** pages!)

"MEDITATIVE BRIDAL RITUAL" OPTION:

How to Use the *RitualWise* Bridal Notes to Create a Personal "Meditative Bridal Ritual"

PREPARATION IDEAS:

• The design of the "meditative bridal ritual" is to select and read one *RitualWise* **Bridal Note** from each of the five rhyme sections, creating a kind of synergetic message for you. In this way, you are interweaving:

1. the **past** (*something old*),
2. the **present** (*something new*),
3. the **future** (*something borrowed*),
4. the **divine** (*something blue*),
5. the **practical** (*a sixpence for your shoe*)

• To mark the pages, perhaps use bits of ribbon from your wedding gift packages that you've opened.

• Whether you do this exercise first thing when you wake up in the morning to set the pace of your day or in the evening for messages to take into your dreams or just whenever you need a little "take a breather" moment—it's the perfect time!

• Perhaps listen to soft music or my *Open Your Heart* Meditation CD for Brides (www.WeddingsOfGrace.com) to take you into a quiet space of inner stillness.

• Find your own rhythm and way to enjoy the **RitualWise Bridal Notes**, incorporating ideas you have to make a little "ritual ceremony" out of the selection and reading process. Remember to slow down, relax as you breathe into your heart center, and take deep easy inhales and long soft exhales. (Practice inhaling and exhaling through your nose for even more relaxation.)

• By participating in the simplicity of this womanly bridal ritual, you will not only expand your own capacity for love, but you will also open a pathway of deeper heart connections for future generations of brides.

TO BEGIN:

1. Find a private moment in your day or evening; settle into a cozy spot with *The Bride's Ritual Guide*. As you nestle into your own "ritual reverie," begin to take deep soft breaths, letting go of your long to-do list. Keep your attention on your breath and allow your body to just drop the weight of busyness, letting the flow of your breath sweep away tension.

2. Close your eyes for a few moments as you continue to take deep easy breaths (inhaling and exhaling through your nose if you can) until you find that soft-spot of quietness within. Delight in the pleasure of being *you*... an open heart will take you there.

3. Allow the rhythm of your breathing to ease you into quiet "ritual time." ("Ritual time" is a meditative-like space that happens when you engage in a process from your inner awareness, trusting your wise spirit—your intuition—to guide you instead of your busy mind trying to figure out what's next!)

4. With soft, deep, slow inhales and long lingering exhales, relax into this quieter still space as you begin to feel your heart open. Here is where your true self emerges. (When you pause and put attention on your breathing, it helps slow down your life to the magic of "ritual time" for a few moments of inner stillness and peacefulness. Your best creative ideas come from this quiet place!)

5. Keep your attention inward and continue your deep relaxing breaths, and when you're ready, select (randomly or in some order if you wish) one *RitualWise* **Bridal Note** from each of the five "something" sections in *The Bride's Ritual Guide* book.

6. Mark the pages with your ribbons like you've discovered a precious gift to your spirit. (And if you only have time for selecting and reading one *RitualWise* **Bridal Note** this go round, that's perfect too!)

7. Pause a moment before reading (silently or aloud) each *RitualWise* **Bridal Note** you selected, giving your deep, easy breaths a chance to open your heart to the messages you find. Each message is perfect for that moment.

8. (One way to deepen the relaxation experience of your "meditative bridal ritual" is to close your eyes and pause after reading each *RitualWise* **Bridal Note**, allowing the words to just be...finding their way into your heart.)

9. Once you've completed your version of the "meditative bridal ritual," use your *Wisdom Journal* inside *The Bride's Ritual Guide* to record any insights and revelations from your experience.

10. Writing this down helps take any openings you had deeper into your heart. (Even if you didn't realize that something opened up for you, I bet it did! Perhaps a bit of journaling will reveal some new awareness.)

11. Now take the sweetness and ease of your personal "meditative bridal ritual" experience into the rest of your day or evening. "*Look inside to find yourself*"...and enjoy the journey.

RitualWise Bridal Notes

SOMETHING OLD

~ Something of remembrance and femininity ~

To connect your life with a legacy of women
who have traveled along this path

~SOMETHING OLD~

No. 1: Each Detail of Your Heart

There's a great deal of romance and juicy energy around the fabled "wedding dress." These *costumes with a past* have become mythical creatures, described as "gowns of ritual" by historian Carol McD. Wallace. Wedding dresses evoke intimate, interlinking stories as women wistfully describe in detail the scoop of a neckline, the pattern of lace, the shape of a sleeve, the whish of a train, but especially how wearing it made them feel. "Every woman should see herself looking uniquely breathtaking, in something tailored to celebrate her body," Susan Jane Gilman exclaims in *Hypocrite in a Pouffy White Dress.*

Wedding dresses—whether you wear something old or something new—connect women in an echoing sisterly heritage. Share with someone how wearing your wedding dress makes/made you feel. Soak in feeling feminine and luscious and gorgeous in your *own* eyes!

These are precious moments that invite you to celebrate your womanliness. And you don't have to wait for your wedding day or stop doing it on your wedding day or even have a wedding day for such a celebration! No, you don't wear a figure-shaping, goddess-inspiring, glowing white ball gown designed to show off your femininity every day, but you *can* celebrate *you* every day—body and spirit!

Women usually remember the moment they first saw themselves in their wedding gown—like seeing a cherished, intimate part of themselves seldom shared with anyone. What will you remember about these "precious moments"? Slow down, there's no rush...savor each detail of your heart. Breathe deeply and easily into your heart center and just hang out there for a bit. And in this soft sweet place, remember the "feeling beautiful" feeling and carry it with you no matter what you are wearing.

~SOMETHING OLD~

No. 2: *Lavender Scented Handkerchief*
(Wedding Hankie, Take One)

Carrying a pretty handkerchief is an old custom that, even today, can inspire our feminine nature. Legends have been created just from stories about a lady's scented handkerchief and her feminine wiles! Victorian ladies kept stems of English lavender in their decorative hankie cases, infusing the handkerchiefs with its relaxing, romantic fragrance. (Then it was always ready to calm excited nerves—perhaps when a special suitor came to call.)

Here's a soothing tip for your wedding day. Buy a pretty but practical linen handkerchief to carry. It can be white or a soft pastel, vintage or new but not too fancy. (Or perhaps your grandmother has one to give you.) When your wedding day comes, scent your "sensible" hankie with a bit of calming lavender essential oil. Keep the scented hankie with you during your wedding activities to have its relaxing fragrance always available.

Remember that being relaxed and at ease brings out your feminine nature. And 'tis okay to share your secret: keep a little bottle of lavender essential oil in your wedding purse for a hankie refresher and even put a drop on *his* handkerchief as well!

· ⟡ ·

You don't have to wait for your wedding day—breathe in some of that lavender-scented magic right now! Do this little exercise: Close your eyes, take a couple of deep soothing breaths, inhaling and exhaling through your nose if possible, and then visualize a time you felt feminine through and through—and breathe in that strength, beauty, and confidence. It's always there, always available for you to claim. Relax and breathe it in.

~SOMETHING OLD~

No. 3: *Don't Go Down the Aisle Without One*
(Wedding Hankie, Take Two)

Let's have a serious girl-to-girl chat! As modern and savvy as you are, you know that sometimes "old-fashioned" is the way to go. So be sure to have a "serviceable" handkerchief with you during your wedding ceremony. It's perhaps the most sensible and practical thing you can do on your wedding day: for tears, a runny nose, damp palms, or for dabbing his moist brow. Trust me…don't go down the aisle without one!

In the days when I had my designer bridal store (where I always kept a stock of "best-selling" pretty vintage handkerchiefs), I went to hundreds of weddings. And the most frequent "mistake" I saw was a bride at the altar without something to discreetly take care of a runny nose. (You don't need an "extra hand" for your hankie. Just tuck it into your palm for easiest access.)

Part of our "feminine smarts" is to be able to take care of the little things gracefully and the big things with even more grace. These practical—and sometimes old-fashioned—things (like having a "serviceable" hankie) can add ease and comfort to nervous times…and make a beautiful bride even more beautiful.

· ·

Weddings are a great opportunity to thank the women in your world for their contributions to your life. Find ways to include women and girls of all ages in your wedding festivities. The strength of female support is like the iconic linen handkerchief—a fine old friend!

~SOMETHING OLD~

No. 4: Treasured Relationships

A bridal gown not only reflects a woman's personal style, but it also speaks eloquently of families and communities, relationship and history. As a treasured family inheritance, bridal attire is saved to share with future generations: from bits of lace and ribbon to the entire wedding ensemble. (Are you wearing something for your wedding that is a valued family heirloom?)

Through the years, I have visited dozens of popular exhibitions at museums around the world featuring bridal costumes and accessories, revealing an anthropologist-like view into the heart of a particular community. At times during my visits, it's as though I can *feel* the relationships infused in the wedding garments: mother-daughter, daughter-father, friend to friend, beloved to beloved, woman to her culture. The universal appeal of these exhibits shows how bridal paraphernalia provides pleasure and memories, contributing to people's lives long after the initial wearing, long beyond the ceremony's end.

Weddings are undeniably about relationships, even including the bride's relationship with her special dress—which can get a bit obsessive at times. California photographer Leslie Barton remarked, "It seems to me the gown is really the guest of honor. It is treated with a delicacy and respect that few humans experience."

Dear Bride: Love your dress, treasure how it makes you feel, celebrate your day, honor your heritage, and treat all of your wedding guests as the "guest of honor"!

Relationships are also part of our "treasured inheritance," and they come in all shapes and sizes: some easy to embrace and other relationships in need of a bit of "mending." Wedding planning time—the scheduling, the parties, even the wedding day itself—is a perfect opportunity to tend to that mending! Reach out...love, listen, forgive, and let go.

~SOMETHING OLD~

No. 5: *Veiled in Legendary Mystery* (Bridal Veil, Take One)

I have a collection of old wedding photographs from the late nineteenth and early twentieth centuries of brides wearing their "best dress"—usually a dark color. To make her dark outfit more festive and "bridal," some brides wore fresh flowers or wax orange blossoms in their hair with some sort of veil attached. The veil seemed to declare, "I'm a bride!"

What has come to be known as a "bridal veil" in European-American heritage—now synonymous with the "white wedding"—has its own unique story. Modern veils borrow the best from both Eastern and Western cultural backgrounds. From Eastern tradition, brides inherit a sense of being veiled as capturing a meditative space for their own private reverie. The Western lineage of the veil takes inspiration from the prestige and grandeur of fashions from life at royal court.

Like a lot of things in our lives, the magic is in the *balance* of it all. In the bridal veil tradition, that balance is *introspection with beauty*. Modern brides—blessed to have such a lovely heritage—have a passel of choices at their fingertips to express their own bridal mystique. Wear the mystery well and become part of the legend!

Even if you don't wear a bridal veil, you are "veiled" in legendary mystery on your wedding day. You are stepping into the past touched by women of the ages, offering a bit of themselves as a way to contribute to your life. Reach out to receive their blessings and share them with the next in line.

~SOMETHING OLD~

No. 6: The Veil Reveals the Woman (Bridal Veil, Take Two)

"'My veil was magical. And so simple. Just one layer of tulle about six feet long. It floated in the wind as I walked down the aisle,'" a bride expresses in the charming book *The Bride Revealed*. When I had my bridal art-to-wear store years ago, I encouraged the bride to wear a veil—it seemed to complete the ritual of her costume, and I knew she would love how it made her feel. This was during a time when wearing a veil was sometimes a more vague choice, even misunderstood, but always slightly mysterious.

I also liked how wearing a veil created a rather ethereal quality, bringing a lovely stillness to the bride's presence, supporting her inner transformation. As I dressed and fitted brides in the intimacy of my shop, I shared this impression: *Imagine the bridal veil as representing the mystery of womanhood. Wrapped in a gossamer cloud, the veil reveals the woman!*

Then some enchantment would always follow. As I attached a veil to the headpiece in the bride's hair, I watched closely as she turned to her image in the mirror. Her eyes widened, her face softened, her heart opened and then a little gasp as she looked at her reflection, like some long lost recognition remembered.

. . . . ⌘ . . . .

What would you like revealed during this rather mysterious and womanly rite-of-passage you are moving through? It's a journey into a deeper part of your true self...just imagine the possibilities to be "unconcealed." Look inside to your awareness. Your heart's desire is waiting to speak to you.

~SOMETHING OLD~

No. 7: Return to Love

Inheriting the blessings from the first owner, some brides wear gowns that have been *recreated* just for them: their mother or grandmother's dress, a restored vintage dress, or a "gently worn" gown from a consignment store. These are dresses with a little bit of past that get to shine again with a few changes, as beautiful as ever.

Even a new gown usually needs some nips 'n tucks to make it work just for you. It's like love; you have to *recreate* its essence for each new appearance. (And sometimes love requires *you* to adjust for a "better fit" as well.)

Whether or not *your* gown is ever worn again (and you may never know), be sure to add your own special blessings just in case. And in some mystical way, those blessings come back to you.

A wedding gown—whether new, old, or borrowed—holds a womanly legacy. Pause and notice how beautiful you feel in your wedding gown—from the "inside out"—and let that feeling seep deep into your bones. Relish it. Breathe in the feeling of beauty and womanliness. Remember how it feels so you can return to this sweet place. Make a note in your *Wisdom Journal* about your impressions. Pause...don't miss this moment to return to love.

~SOMETHING OLD~

No. 8: Leaving Blessings in Her Wake

Wearing a gown with a train has such a fairy tale quality. I enjoyed watching brides-to-be trying on gowns in my former shop as they twirled and turned in front of the mirror, craning their necks like some exotic bird attempting to see how their train magically draped and "puddled" behind them.

During this "mirror ritual," I shared a pretty notion with each bride, embellishing a quote from former editor in chief of *Bride's* magazine, Barbara Tober: *The train of the gown is an extension of the presence of the bride…on her wedding day she moves amongst her friends and family, leaving blessings in her wake.* (Pause here, and as you take an easy deep breath, simply let your imagination play with that image for a moment.)

Weddings offer many opportunities to leave loving blessings trailing behind your bright aura! How do you intend to make your wedding a ritual of love for everyone present?

. . . .

A wedding gown does not a bride make! I've worked with brides of all ages—from seventeen to eighty-seven, from first marriage to more than three—and every bride is lit with a "fairy tale quality" no matter what she was wearing. Perhaps new love does that: lights you up from within, surrounds you with blessings, raises you above the mundane.

What do you need to put into place so you don't lose, or at least so you can recapture, that "lit from within feeling" *after* the wedding…when life becomes "normal"? Look inside to find *your* magic.

~SOMETHING OLD~

No. 9: The Fragrance of Love

In bridal folklore, the fragrant orange blossom became legendary. Native to China and one of the rare plants that blooms and bears fruit at the same time, the orange tree's aromatic flowers became symbolic of fruitfulness and fertility. Inspired by the legend as well as its glorious scent, ancient brides in Mediterranean countries wrapped the creamy white blossoms and delicate greenery into nuptial halos. All wedding rituals are rooted in this hopeful promise of the continuity of life that the orange blossom epitomizes.

Whatever flowers you wear or carry on your wedding day—mixing nature's fragrances and textures—they are beautiful reminders of that promise of abundance. Life follows life, and love makes it all worthwhile. Here's a suggestion; give some of your wedding flowers to a little girl to take home with her...continuing the legacy and the love.

Weddings are full of folklore and legends. Perhaps that's part of the mystery that draws us to them...as well as the appealing possibility of love forever. And flowers seem to hold the essence of that magic. I've had brides tell me that when they've gotten nervous getting ready to walk down that long aisle, they focused on their bouquet for a moment— taking in its beauty, breathing in its scent—then relaxed and settled back into knowing everything was okay.

Try it right now...take a deep slow breath, breathing in the soothing fragrance of love!

~SOMETHING OLD~

*N*o. 10: *Be a Goddess for a Lifetime* (Goddess, Take One)

The tradition of the white wedding gown is neither universal, nor is it very old. Queen Victoria of England, at her wedding in 1840, was not the first bride to wear white, but her grand influence set the "bridal white" fashion in motion…and the rest is history.

Wearing white has always had a ceremonial and regal quality, for whatever occasion, taking on a kind of radiance. In my costume history research exploring goddess mythology, I find a heritage of shimmering white gowns worn by ancient luminous deities who embodied the female essence of beauty, strength, and love. Goddesses all! Perhaps then, as a bride, you are indeed the "epiphany of the goddess." *Hmmm*…try that on for a moment. Then allow that goddess awareness to draw you closer to your own feminine nature and breathe in its soulful beauty.

. . . .

Whatever you wear for your wedding—a white gown, a colorful kimono, or a pair of jeans—you carry something of the goddess spirit with you! Your ritual costume wraps you in a bit of "royal lineage" that now simply becomes a part of who you are. As I've told brides for years, *Don't settle for being a "princess for a day"—be a "goddess for a lifetime."*

Something New

~ Something of possibility and self-discovery ~

The aliveness of being truly present to love in each moment

PHOTOGRAPH BY PRISCILLA WANNAMAKER

~SOMETHING NEW~

No. 1: *The Eyes of Love*

Throughout the ages, poets have described the eyes as reflections of the heart. Songwriters wax eloquently about a more radiant world seen through the eyes of love. Indeed, your love shines from your eyes... it's hard to hide it. "The love light in her eye," as English poet Hartley Coleridge describes.

Let's see if we can light up those lovely eyes of yours even more! Yoga masters teach "breathing through the eyes" as a way toward deep relaxation, a visualization technique to regroup mentally, physically, and emotionally. Try this for a few minutes: close your eyes; as you take deep, slow inhales and breathe out with even slower exhales, imagine your breath flowing in and out of your *eyes*; refreshing, cleansing, relaxing.

When you are more at ease, there is more of *you* available to express love and acceptance. Allow each breath you take to open your heart... and then every deep breath opens a whole new world where you hear, feel, and *see* more. So, *Ms. Bright Eyes*, let your love light shine!

Visualize someone or something you love...then breathe that image in "through your eyes" and into your heart. As you take deep easy breaths, let the imagination of your "mind's eye" have its playful way! Feel the pleasure of your refreshing breath, and as you slowly breathe out, imagine your exhales as mysterious, romantic sighs. (A girl needs a little mystery every now and then to give poets something to write about!)

~SOMETHING NEW~

No. 2: Look to Your Awareness

Being a conscious bride takes courage. You step into a spotlight when you become a bride, emotions bubble up during this busy time, perhaps self-doubt creeps in. However, it's the design of a rite-of-passage to shake you up a bit, to prepare you for a huge leap of faith. This may be unsettling at first, yet it is the nature of change…to inspire an inner awakening, to prepare you for unconditional love.

Then how do you keep yourself centered and open? How do you stay settled in your own skin so you can efficiently and thoughtfully handle your growing to-do list? To stay true to your heart, connected to your relationship, and focused on the spirit of love, "look to your awareness, not to your thoughts," *Conversations with God* author Neale Donald Walsch counsels. "Your thoughts about things can betray you—and often do—because they can be colored by emotions. Your awareness cannot."

Look to your awareness, your inner self. Don't give your noisy, full-of-drama thoughts any attention; just let them pass through like a tipsy wedding guest. You have more important things to take care of: focusing on what lights you up, sharing yourself with a friend, manifesting your heart's desire. That's the nature of a conscious bride. It makes the trip deeper, sweeter, and just more fun!

. . . .

Use this time in the bridal spotlight to find your quiet center and ground yourself. Have a gentle, meditative stretching routine of some sort that helps relax your body and supports your inner peacefulness. From that more settled aware place, your mind gets quieter; your emotions won't be so apt to bubble over; you become less reactive, more responsive, more creative, more conscious, more available for love.

~SOMETHING NEW~

No. 3: *Listen to Your Heart*

Take a private quiet moment to listen to your heart each day. "The hub of your calmness," as Elizabeth Gilbert calls one's heart in *Eat, Pray, Love*. What's the message you hear? Listen deep into the stillness so the message can get through. Fine-tune your heart radio! Allow yourself to let love in from all directions and from all of life's voices. What do you hear in the background? (Remember that the magic of life is sometimes in the background, so pay attention.) Everyone's heart is speaking to you. Their hearts' voice is *your* heart's voice that was there all along.

When the wedding planning bustle spins you away from yourself and you're feeling a bit frazzled, what do you do to ease back into your heart center? Close your eyes and take a few deep, soft breaths and listen in. Listen for what soothes and supports your best self. When you find the quiet inside, you realize you're not alone…your inner spirit is always there to guide and nurture you.

. . . .

Sometimes it's not easy to find that quiet moment of contemplation in your day or evening. However, your spirit calls for it! Take a walk in the park, in the woods, down the street, along a lane, beside a lake. Go sit by a tree…or at least by yourself for a few moments of quiet each day. (A closet will do!) And listen for love.

~SOMETHING NEW~

No. 4: Use Your Soft Eyes

Planning your wedding is a busy time, yes? You tend to "hard focus" when you get busy: concentrating, figuring things out, trying to remember a myriad of facts and details. Not only does such hard focus strain your eyes, making you tired, but you are also less present, which means there's less of *you* available to connect with others.

So when you are reading or using the computer or talking with someone or just sitting there thinking about your wedding plans, practice "soft focus." Soft focus allows your eyes to *relax* in their sockets, instead of pushing them out. No effort, no force, no straining.

Try it now. Notice if you're squinting or if you're feeling tightness around your eyes. Gently open your eyes a little wider, just what feels natural. Let go of any tension and imagine your eyeballs floating unattached in their sockets. *Hmmm.* It feels kind of dreamy, doesn't it? Keep practicing…it relaxes and softens your whole face. In fact, relaxing your eyes helps soften all of life's edges.

Now go out 'n about with your "dreamy eyes"—and remember that soft eyes just naturally encourage a soft loving heart. Take care of yourself first; then details of your wedding will just fall "softly" into place.

· ❧ ·

From ancient wisdom, each part of the body has its own particular energy; and the iris of the eye, it is said, relates to love. As your eyes are more rested and less tense, your irises begin returning to their natural round full shape. (*Ahhhh*…more love can get in.)

"Soft focus" your way through wedding planning…and see how beautiful people are through your *soft eyes of love*. Plus, *you* will look like a dream!

~SOMETHING NEW~

No. 5: *Stay Present to Love*

After the months of planning, after the final words of the ceremony, after the last toast of the reception, after stepping out of your wedding gown, after your wedding day is complete—what *image* do you want to remain in the imagination of your wedding guests? How do you want to be remembered—happy, serene, gorgeous, sexy, "at one with the universe"?

What really remains unforgettable and inspiring is not just the vision of a lovely woman in a beautiful dress, but the image of a woman with her heart open, grounded in her love and expressing it freely. Now, that's not only breathtaking but also inspires others to open their own heart a wee bit more.

Being grounded comes with taking deep slow breaths, finding your quiet center, listening for your inner voice, getting deeply rooted in your true nature, and claiming your magnificence. Serenity comes with loving first and letting go of whatever is in the way of expressing that love. Take people's breath away—stay present to love. You'll be a knockout!

~SOMETHING NEW~

No. 6: Love What You Choose

There are so many choices to make when you're a bride-to-be, but good news! A woman's intuition seems to light up as a bride. That's just part of the mystical nature of a rite-of-passage. (And why so many brides find *the* dress during their first round of shopping!) The more aware you are, the more you can tap into your inner resources where your intuitive "wise self" lives. So don't resist…enjoy the ease that comes with following your "inner wise-woman."

Your time as a bride-to-be becomes a perfect opportunity to listen to that instinctive wisdom inside you, allowing it to guide your choices—foregoing doubt and second-guessing. (I think I read this on a greeting card: *Worrying about the past or the future just saps today of its magic!*)

Here's what your wise inner voice is telling you when it comes to making a choice: *Choose from your heart's desire, then love what you choose. Move on to the next decision, and choose…then love that.* You get the picture. Choose it, love it, move on! Let the love flow.

. . . .

Be patient with yourself during this busy time, and don't let frustration take over. Trust your intuition and keep your vision on the bigger picture—your well-being and your relationship—and allow the love and support you find there be a buoy for you. What you need will show up at the perfect time.

Here's a tip: Use the power of your breath and take a thoughtful pause before making a decision. Breathe deeply and slowly (inhaling and exhaling through your nose when you can); let your breath settle you, and in that quiet space, *pause*. Inside that pause is the *here and now*…the present moment…a gift…all you need to know…the perfect *you*. Now, choose with love.

~SOMETHING NEW~

No. 7: *Tending to Your Heart*

Sometimes it's hard not to lose yourself when planning your wedding. There are so many distractions vying for your attention that not only can it become rather daunting, making you a bit dizzy, but you can also lose your connection to your relationship. So how do you keep your cool, your heart open, and your attention on what matters? Before you look "out there" at the smorgasbord of choices, look *inside* to get centered.

Just taking some deep, easy breaths and slowing down for a few minutes when you feel the swirl coming on makes a huge difference in your well-being—and in his! Remember that "energy follows attention," so keep your attention on the things you love. And of course, your relationship is at the top of the list. (That's your relationship with yourself and with your partner.) When you're tending to your own heart, you are tending to his. When you are tending to his heart, you are tending to your own.

Since the spotlight is on the bride, keep *your* spotlight on *him*! Leave little "*I love you*" post-it notes around in "hidden" places for him to find. Sharing love is soothing and energizing all at the same time. Soothing frayed edges, energizing well-being. As English poet Philip James Bailey reminds us: "*Love spends his all, and still hath store.*"

~SOMETHING NEW~

No. 8: Deep Breathing

Give yourself the gift of relaxation during everyday moments. While looking at bridal magazines, wrapping presents, or writing thank-you notes, pay attention to your breathing. Begin inhaling and exhaling with a soft, deep, languid rhythm. Breathing guru Dennis Lewis reminds us: "Sense the natural pause after exhalation; let yourself rest there for a moment." Notice the difference it makes…you'll begin to feel more settled, more centered, more *you*.

To deepen the relaxation even more, play soothing music in the background or use headphones for more intimacy when you're doing these kinds of solitary tasks. Then in addition to accomplishing stuff, it becomes a relaxing, meditative time to boot!

While you're at it, give your body some attention. Where in your body are you tense, tight, contracted, or clenched up? Take a slow, deep inhaling breath into that area of your body; gently wiggle it around if it's "wiggleble," then turn your exhale into a long, soft humming sigh as you imagine the tightness and tension melting from your head to your toes.

Ahhhh…life just got less complicated.

Right now as you are reading this, notice your breathing. Is it shallow or perhaps you're even holding your breath! Remember to breatheeeeeeeee. My friend and Feldenkrais instructor Lavinia Plonka suggests, "If you notice you're not breathing, then hold your breath for a couple of counts and let your body remember."

Slow it all down. Take pleasure in slow motion, "molasses in January" kind of deep easy breathing. This helps you relax and a more relaxed bride-to-be is a more beautiful bride!

~SOMETHING NEW~

No. 9: *Your Inner Smile* (Smile, Take One)

The world knows about your big beautiful smile, but did you know that you had an "inner smile" as well? Let's see if we can find it: Take deep, slow breaths as you put your attention inside; feel the soft caress of your breath moving through you; appreciate this yummy moment and breathe a smile into your heart, allowing something still and sweet to surface. Wise sages tell us that "love is breathing into your heart." Close your eyes and continue your deep, relaxing *heart breathing* for a few moments.

Does that feel like an inner smile? It sure looks like it from over here...like an open smiling heart! Radiant brides have radiant *inner smiles*.

. . . .

Smiling helps release tension and brings you back to yourself. Smiling relaxes the body, slows down your breaths, quiets your thoughts, radiates warmth and connection, and creates the world anew. It's hard to be angry or jealous or "pissy" with a big smile on your face. So...smile, Girl, smile!

~SOMETHING NEW~

No. 10: Love and Gratitude

On your wedding day, set aside a bit of "just for you" meditative time to center yourself and get grounded: by listening to music, stretching gently, reading a favorite poem, or doing a soothing deep-breathing exercise. As you relax during this little "wedding day reverie," the world gets quieter and your inner voice can be heard. Be grateful for everything that comes up—yes, even that! Don't stuff anything back down; just breathe love into it.

Easy does it. Relax more deeply and allow your body to remember that sweet moment of "falling in love"—breathe in the feeling so you can recreate it fresh and new—and take that feeling with you throughout your wedding day. Share it with friends, family, strangers. Like love, weddings are about inclusion. Be the *goddess* of love today!

Love and gratitude are intertwined. Many people supported you to get to this place today. Perhaps you've thanked them all, but saying "I love you" sometimes is more difficult—to some it's easy, to others maybe not. So remember, love without forgiveness is not love. Let it go! Let your wedding day be a day where saying "I love you" just slips off your tongue. "Thank you. I love you." "I love you. Thank you." (See how easy it is?)

SOMETHING BORROWED

~ Something precious and full of grace ~

PHOTOGRAPH BY PRISCILLA WANNAMAKER

~SOMETHING BORROWED~

No. 1: *Borrowing from the Past*

Wedding ceremonies "borrow" from the past—words, music, gestures—and when you participate in wedding rituals, you are "borrowing" wisdom from another time. As you tap into those ancient wisdoms, you are tapping into your own *inner* wisdom. That's why when you're going through these intimate rituals, it can all feel *strangely* natural and familiar . . . *"Have I been here before?"* It's not the ritual itself; rituals are just a vehicle to take you into your heart center. What is familiar is *you!* The real you gets to emerge.

The most memorable wedding ceremonies draw the best from the past yet become beautifully *present*. Therefore, whatever you "borrow" to create your wedding, stir it up with your own inspired magic so it comes *from* your heart! Borrowing it from the past, giving it your *presence*.

. . . .

Take time now to write in your *Wisdom Journal*...perhaps some new awareness. Let the words just fall onto the page—coming from your heart's desire—and see what magic appears! It may be just what you needed to hear (and wisdom that a future bride-to-be needs to "borrow"). Whether it's participating in wedding rituals or journaling or meditating—it's all a process to get you back to *you*!

~SOMETHING BORROWED~

No. 2: Honoring the Lineage of Women

For thousands of years in cultures worldwide, young girls were taught the art of needlework. Like a girl in the Black Miao villages in southwest China or in the Rabari communities in northwest India where she might spend the early years of her girlhood embroidering her wedding costume.

But societies change, and today these girls—perhaps more skilled with a computer keyboard than with a needle—borrow their elaborate wedding costume from village elders. The world may change, but women always love to connect in rituals of the heart, sharing their talents to champion another woman.

As you're planning your wedding, share something with your attendants in the spirit of this vibrant lineage. It doesn't have to a physical object; it can be a story from your own heritage, remembrances of women you know or read about, or a hug that says "thank you from my heart." Share *yourself.*

Few women today make their wedding gown or stitch their trousseau, but it doesn't mean that you don't *weave* your heart's desire into your wedding finery! Whether you borrow a locket or brooch or tiara from another woman for your wedding—or even if everything you wear is brand-new—you borrow skills and patience and courage from the lineage of women. Wear whatever you wear to honor that heritage.

~SOMETHING BORROWED~

No. 3: *Keep the Borrowed Wisdom Flowing*

Keep *The Bride's Ritual Guide* with you. Remember to jot down in the *Wisdom Journal* section any insights noticed along your wedding planning journey. Get into a rhythm where you're using your *Wisdom Journal* on a regular basis to help anchor your heart experiences.

Here's an idea. At any moment when you have a chance—especially when tired or tense—do this little harmonizing exercise: Get comfy and as you close your eyes, begin softly inhaling then slowly exhaling through your nose (it's more relaxing). When you're ready, on the first exhale of three deep slow breaths, relax your shoulders. Take your time and on the next exhale, relax your neck. On the third deep lazy exhale, relax your jaw. As you open your eyes, continuing to take calming deep breaths, turn to a quotation page in your *Wisdom Journal* and read the "message" waiting for you there. Sometimes we just need to "borrow" a little wisdom-ease!

Today, call or e-mail someone that you haven't been in touch with for a while and share what you love about planning your wedding, or what you are noticing about yourself during the process, or share a favorite quotation from your *Wisdom Journal*. Keep the "borrowed" wisdom flowing!

And if you're feeling stuck or overwhelmed, share that with someone as a way to breathe ease into the tension. It helps. Invite your attendants to "attend" to your well-being. This is a time to be nurtured. Request support—even *Superwoman* called on friends!

~SOMETHING BORROWED~

No. 4: Less Is More

There are more and more eco-friendly ideas available to inspire "eco-chic" weddings: using recyclable materials, organic flowers, reusable decorations. Here's a twist. Your "something borrowed" could mean using flowers from a friend's backyard, linens from an aunt for the reception, serving utensils and vases from neighbors. "Be a champion of recycling," Emily Elizabeth Anderson prompts us in her book, *Eco-Chic Weddings*.

It's easy to let weddings get a bit over-the-top, but there is a growing awareness—once again—that *less is more*. "Borrowing" thoughtful values from simpler times…it just feels good, don't you think?

. . . .

However simple or elaborate your wedding becomes, keep your level head, your big heart, and your generous spirit! Don't be afraid to say, *"Hang on. Let's rethink that idea. Is there a simpler way to do that? Is there a more 'green' solution here? What are ways to be inclusive without inviting everyone to everything?"* In wedding celebrations—small, grand, or somewhere in-between—thoughtful is always "chic."

~ SOMETHING BORROWED ~

No. 5: Treasured Words

Words have magic and power to them. Words that you and your partner consider for your wedding vows are treasured "borrowed wisdom." You may choose sacred words from an old religious text or something from your ancient heritage, like the Cherokee Wedding Prayer or Celtic Blessings, or perhaps from literature, such as Shakespeare's Sonnets. Whatever source you borrow from…the words are a gift. Even if you write your own vows, these are words that have resonated with other ageless lovers searching for that perfect expression of the heart.

As you speak the words of declaration at your wedding, don't rush. Allow their energy and rhythm to flow deep inside you, feel them in your heart, moving you to a new place of love and commitment.

During the "busyness" of wedding planning, why don't you and your partner choose favorite love poems to read to each other as a way to stay connected? Close your eyes if you're the one listening; gently deepen your breathing; and as the words are spoken, see if you can *feel* them in your body.

Practice 'til you can tell the difference in "hearing" the words and "feeling" the words. Bring that distinction to your wedding day vows and feel them in your heart.

~SOMETHING BORROWED~

No. 6: The Lingering Pleasure of a Pause

"Borrow" favorite poems and quotations and add them to your **Wisdom Journal**, collecting them as memorable messages to mark this special time. Then borrow a technique from seasoned public speakers: the intentional pause. Here's a way to practice. Slowly and out loud, read one of the poems or other additions in your **Wisdom Journal** to yourself or a friend with a deliberate *pause* between each phrase. What did you notice? Was it easy or hard to slow down? Did you want to rush and fill the silence?

Practice some more. Find *yourself* in the spaces as you read. Give the words breathing room...and continue to find the grace in the *pauses*. Life becomes sweeter when it's a practice of what gently serves love instead of a rush to the finish line!

. . . .

This will be great practice for your wedding day: to slow down and find the luscious *spaces* in your words...in your steps...in your hugs and embraces. Enjoy the *lingering* pleasure of each moment, of each pause. It's okay to slow down. You will get to the wedding altar—or wherever your journey takes you—at the perfect moment.

~ SOMETHING BORROWED ~

No. 7: A Borrowed Keepsake

Borrowing a piece of jewelry or a handbag or headpiece from a friend or family member for your wedding day provides you blessings from them as well as a beautiful accessory to use. Continue the tradition. Offer another bride-to-be an item from *your* wedding, perhaps for her "something borrowed." However, if she already has all she needs, it's okay; you are offering her your blessings, and they are a *keepsake* forever.

Sometimes what is offered is more of a symbol, more ephemeral, yet deeply personal and heartfelt. Carol McD. Wallace recounts in her book *All Dressed in White*, "Each of the women who worked on Princess Elizabeth of England's wedding gown embroidered a strand of her own hair into the gown, as a way of embodying her good wishes for the princess bride." There is no limit to how we can share our love.

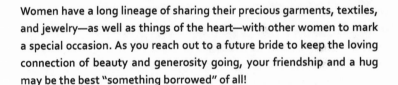

Women have a long lineage of sharing their precious garments, textiles, and jewelry—as well as things of the heart—with other women to mark a special occasion. As you reach out to a future bride to keep the loving connection of beauty and generosity going, your friendship and a hug may be the best "something borrowed" of all!

~SOMETHING BORROWED~

No. 8: *The Goddess Bride* (Goddess, Take Two)

Even if your wedding gown is new, it has roots in the past. Today's bridal "ball gown" styles borrow from thousands of years of fashion design. So you may be wearing a style of gown inspired from something worn by a queen or empress or even a goddess.

Feeling "regal" as a bride is part of your natural inheritance. No wonder that tiaras—elegance borrowed from another time—remain a favorite bridal headpiece today. Throughout history, there have been wedding ceremonies that "crown" the bride and groom, like in the Russian or Greek Orthodox services, symbolizing the "royal" blessings of their wedding day. Undeniably, your wedding costume brings out a bit of princess fantasy—like a little girl playing "dress up"—and combines it with something grown-up and royal like the beautiful *goddess* you are!

My friend Adele Azar-Rucquoi, who wore no wedding gown nor crown but a white silky blouse and flowing pants with a wide-brim straw hat, was a joyful bride at fifty-nine and the essence of the *regalness* of spirit. Adele shares this remembrance in her book for women, *Money as Sacrament*, about walking down the aisle toward her beloved: "One by one I made eye contact with my friends, grinning until my face hurt. Never have I seen them from so *regal* a place!"

Perhaps it's not what you wear on your wedding day but how you wear it. So wear it well, you beautiful *Goddess Bride*! Allow yourself to feel your *regal* femininity down to your toes, taking pleasure in your unique feminine ways of being compassionate, kind, and strong. And remember, a Goddess Bride always keeps her heart open.

~SOMETHING BORROWED~

No. 9: Your Dream Channel

Pay attention to your dreams during your wedding planning time. Since your intuition is heightened during your bridal rite-of-passage, your "dream channel" becomes more open. So "feed" your dreams! Before you go to sleep, jot down in your *Wisdom Journal* what your heart desires and let your subconscious go to work. Keep your *Wisdom Journal* beside your bed to record those messages that come through dreams. (However, you're not really "borrowing" this dream wisdom because those messages come from *your* inner spirit. So dream big!)

- ❖ -

You don't have to *borrow* someone else's dream—create your own! Keep imagining a life of expansive, all-inclusive love and "dream" it true. We are all works in progress...just stay open and ready to *receive*. (And these dreams are yours to *keep*!)

~SOMETHING BORROWED~

No. 10: *What Lights You Up*

As you're planning your wedding, you are probably "borrowing" ideas from magazines and books, friends' weddings, old movies, family heritage—the inspiration is all around! Whatever ideas you borrow, do what lights you up and fills your heart. Beware of the wedding trap that would have you do things because it's what people expect, or it's the latest fashion, or even because it's tradition. Your wedding is an expression of your unique artistry and creativity…and especially your love. What do *you* want? Be strong. Be happy. Be you.

. . . . ✤ . . . .

After days, weeks, months of planning, the wedding day itself may go by in a flash; perhaps it even becomes a blur! Nonetheless, you are creating memories—memories from your wedding intertwine into the lives of the people present and take on a life all their own. Memories may even be a way of "borrowing" this moment's happiness.

Whatever you remember or don't remember about your wedding day—or whatever the future brings—what do you need to *let go of* (disappointment, blame, anything negative) and *make room for* (intimacy, forgiveness, trust) so the memories of love will be infused in your heart forever?

SOMETHING BLUE

~ Something intimate and magical ~

A sweet and tender connection to something divine;
a reminder of the depth and eloquence of love without conditions

~SOMETHING BLUE~

No. 1: True-love Knots

As an old-fashioned symbol of *true love*, create a blue "Love Knot Bow" to wear pinned inside your wedding dress or on your bridal lingerie. Make tiny loops out of narrow blue ribbon for the bow and then tie single loops, known as "true-love knots," in the dangling streamers. English historian Ann Monsarrat tells of an ancient legend that says the Danish phrase, *Trulofa, fidem do* meaning "faith" or "I plight my troth"—a phrase used in early wedding vows—was the origin of the expression "true-love knots." (Like many legends, it's romantic but probably not accurate!)

Centuries ago, a great deal of fuss was made over a "knot of ribbons," called *favours*, assembled by friends of the bride to give to wedding guests. When the custom was fashionable (*wedding favours* were a convention left over from superstitious times), it became a sign of status and honor for the guests to wear the charming bouquet of knotted ribbons on their arm or tucked into their hats after the wedding event.

Ribbons tied in true-love knots decorated Victorian era ephemera in the nineteenth century then showed up again in the 1920s when large, lush bridal bouquets overstuffed with flowers and dripping with love-knot ribbon streamers—sometimes cascading to the floor—were in vogue.

Hmmmm, could one say that *true love* is untying all the knots to your lover's heart?

If your love is indeed "true," then it comes with a heart full of forgiveness. Love can get "knotty" at times; but as wise voices tell us, *when we learn how to forgive, then we learn how to love*.

~SOMETHING BLUE~

No. 2: *Your Bridal Birthright* (Goddess, Take Three)

The color blue has divine connections. Blue is the color associated with *Mary*, mother of Jesus, and with *Brigit*, the Celtic goddess of healing and the arts. Brigit, called the maiden goddess of springtime, was also known as *Bride*—who gave her name to a woman about to wed. Therefore, as a bride, *you* are the namesake of a goddess!

Goddess mythology brings many stories of bridal origins and connections of the heart. In her book, *The Ancient British Goddess*, Kathy Jones includes this reference in her many goddess tales: "*Bride* is symbolically a horse goddess and her consort, the young god, is depicted as her *groom*, lavishly attending her." Well, then—it's confirmed! Being a bride not only comes with its own legends, but it also comes with your goddess birthright of being lovingly *attended*. Weave this mystical legacy, as Shakespeare expressed "with blue of heaven's own tinct," into your heart and feel its divine connection.

. . . . ⚜ . . . .

Use your time well in the *legendary* bridal spotlight. Start or continue practices that take care of *you*...mind, body, and soul. Journaling, eating healthy foods, doing fun exercises, breathing deeper. This helps keep your mind clear, your body vibrant, and your heart open to receive and give love. It's just naturally what a *goddess* would do!

~SOMETHING BLUE~

No. 3: The Sapphire Mythology

Some brides wear a sapphire ring or pin as their wedding day "something blue." Sapphires have a great deal of ethereal meaning in the world of gemstones. Queen Victoria wore a large sapphire brooch, a gift from her beloved Albert, pinned to her white silk satin gown the day they married. As a teenage bride-to-be, Lady Diana Spencer chose a sapphire and diamond engagement ring from the selection offered her by Prince Charles and the royal family.

The blue sapphire is considered the stone of "holy blessings" and has long symbolized truth, sincerity, and faithfulness. A precious gemstone may not be able to guarantee the love we want, but "holy blessings" come in all shapes and sizes and disguises! Whatever gemstone you wear, it's more of a treasure when you add self-love—a blessing that keeps sharing riches of the heart.

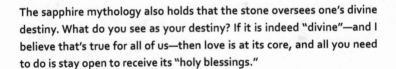

The sapphire mythology also holds that the stone oversees one's divine destiny. What do you see as your destiny? If it is indeed "divine"—and I believe that's true for all of us—then love is at its core, and all you need to do is stay open to receive its "holy blessings."

~SOMETHING BLUE~

No. 4: Be Gentle With Yourself

Historically, all colors have unique properties. Pale blue, known as heaven's blue, is associated with tranquility, softness, and wise understanding. So take your cue from the "something blue" you wear for your wedding and be gentle with yourself. Relax, breathe deeply into your heart, allow your breath to center you, feel your heart open…then give it permission to open even more!

Practice this as you plan your wedding, wrapping yourself in the tranquil spirit of your blue bridal color until its soothing nature becomes just second nature to you. Then that ease will be available to call on long after your wedding when you are in the "routine of life," without as much pomp and ceremony but still with some strain and stress. Here in the every day, you'll welcome a breath of ease and tranquility.

Gently take a deep breath, inhaling the peaceful color of heaven; slowly exhale, breathing out tensions and fear. Make this declaration: *"I'm replacing what doesn't serve me with love and inclusion."* And be true to that little bit of blue heaven!

~SOMETHING BLUE~

No. 5: *The Language of Love*

In Ayurvedic wisdom, the color blue is linked with the throat chakra—or energy center—and inspires balance in our true self-expression. Did you ever think that wearing your bridal "something blue" could support you in being more articulate and eloquent? If that's the case, then being a bride is a perfect time for a powerful declaration of clarity: *"I freely express my thoughts and feelings. I always communicate clearly and effectively."* With clarity comes a stronger sense of purpose. Honor your word, speak your truth, live your purpose, inspire eloquence.

· ❦ ·

Your bridal rite-of-passage has a natural flow and rhythm to it...and when you "get in the zone" of its vibrant energy, the experience deeply supports your inner growth, helping you discover your true strength and power. Here's a tip: if you remember to speak the language of love, then you'll always know where your real power lives.

~SOMETHING BLUE~

No. 6: Take a Breather

Find a pretty piece of blue ribbon (perhaps recycled from your wedding presents), scent it with a drop of soothing lavender essential oil, and use it as a bookmark for the *RitualWise* **Bridal Notes** and *Wisdom Journal* pages. Then each time you open *The Bride's Ritual Guide*, take a deep relaxing breath and say a little blessing for all the people who have guided you to this tender place of love. And soon, as though "out of the blue," love comes back to you on the wings of angels.

. . . .

A heavenly blessing to breathe in right this moment: *"I deeply inhale and bring light into my body; I slowly exhale and feel my body relax, bringing me closer to my inner spirit. I deeply inhale and exhale and offer blessings both ways."* Keep this breathing prayer with you so you can use it anytime you need to "take a breather." (Write it down in your *Wisdom Journal* as though you are handcrafting a promise to yourself!)

~SOMETHING BLUE~

No. 7: Smile Away the Blues (Smile, Take Two)

Okay, so being a bride is not always full of fun and delight. Planning a wedding can become overwhelming, and you just might "get the blues" sometimes. Here's a little secret about feeling better in the moment from a wise woman affectionately known to many as Dr. DooLady: *"What you do is simply turn up the corners of your mouth as if you were smiling. The mind translates that as being happy—as in, 'Oh, we're smiling, I think that means we must be happy!'"*

See how fast this little smiling mind trick can lift your spirits until you're remembering how much you have to appreciate, how much you are loved, how much you really have to smile about!

. . . .

The "blues" are heavy, but smiling lightens the heart and lights up the world around you. Smile as you breathe in and out slowly, deeply and with grateful pleasure—and change your world on the spot! Smiling away *your* blues just may get a little grin from others. So be generous and give the world a gift—smile.

~SOMETHING BLUE~

No. 8: Your Blue Magic

Here's a little *"something blue"* poetic notion just for brides. If indeed blue is a color of divinity; and the queenly blue sapphire is considered a stone of creative expression, intuition, and meditation; and a rite-of-passage is a time of introspection—then if you combine all this "blue magic," you get something rather heavenly! The time of being a bride just naturally becomes ideal to begin or expand a meditative practice to bring ease into your mind, body, and spirit.

A regular meditation practice doesn't have to be complicated or long. Start out with just two minutes of sitting in quietness and work up to perhaps twenty minutes every day. Be patient. You will indeed be touched by a little bit of something divine.

Ahhhh…peaceful stillness awaits you…it's always available in the quiet within. Just take an easy deep breath, "look inside to find yourself," and there *you* are!

Blue is your bride-to-be color…invite it in as a familiar supportive friend. Whenever you use your favorite mug or change your sheets or walk in a garden or look toward heaven—whenever you see blue—let it be a hint to give yourself a gift. A gift of some quiet time each day or evening… listening inward for the stillness where your inner spirit lives. Remember to add this natural *creative expression* to your time as a bride. It's part of your unique "blue magic."

~SOMETHING BLUE~

No. 9: True Blue Love

The expression "true blue"—meaning loyal and unwavering in one's support—comes from the Middle Ages where in Coventry, England, a manufacturer's blue cloth had a reputation for not fading; the color stayed "true." In the world of love and commitment, what's the nature of being "true blue"? Staying true to your word...staying true to your heart...staying true to yourself.

Even when affection, connection, or attention fades, you can always return to love to find your direction. Love has many colors but perhaps only one truth. How do *you* express true love?

Take this moment to have a little "check-in" with your heart. How can you create love that is even more *"true blue"*? What needs to be said or done? Perhaps an apology or just be in touch with someone to restore your heart connection. Say the "hard stuff" with love and stay true to your soft, strong self. Gentle words are courageous words and have a certain strength to them.

~SOMETHING BLUE~

No. 10: An Exchange of Hearts

Folktales abound with stories of the romantic blue *forget-me-not*... the delicate flower that seems to reflect the color of the sky. In the charming language of flowers—where meanings are assigned to flowers and herbs—the forget-me-not speaks of *human longing for loyalty and lastingness*. No wonder that through the ages, poets speak of this captivating flower assisting people in having their heart's desire.

What is your heart's desire? Ask yourself that question, especially whenever you feel a little "off"...and be honest, be *loyal* to yourself. If your desire is hard to express, then look deeper and let whatever is in your heart spill forth like so many forget-me-nots from a *secret garden*! What shows up may not only get you back on track, but something abundant will grow from it.

Blue was the favorite color of my grandmother, Gummie, and flowers were her passion. She always wore something blue, matching her eyes. Every Sunday during the winter, when camellias were in season, she picked one from her spacious yard and pinned it on the lapel of her dark blue wool coat to wear to church. And without fail, she gave it away, happily pinning the regal purply pink flower on the costume of a beaming recipient. As a little girl watching this gesture, I always felt I was in the charmed presence of something divine—an *exchange of hearts*.

Maybe all flowers are "forget-me-nots"—a sweet reminder to share our love. Give love away, and your heart's desire magically appears.

A SIXPENCE FOR YOUR SHOE

~ Something rich with relationship ~

A grounded life full of gratitude and true abundance

PHOTOGRAPH BY PRISCILLA WANNAMAKER

~A SIXPENCE FOR YOUR SHOE~

No. 1: Count Your Blessings

If you can't find an old sixpence coin to use for your wedding, perhaps you can find a penny minted the year you were born or a shiny new one that promises "a gracious plenty." Whether you use an old or new coin as a *bridal token* for your wedding day, remember that it's only a *token*. True abundance is a full heart of love…love that you give away *unconditionally*; it's a heart that stays open…ready to receive the love back a hundred times over.

Keep your wedding coin—your token of abundance—tucked away in your jewelry case or keepsake box so it's a reminder of all the riches in your life. And every time you make notes in your wedding planner or jot inspirations in your ***Wisdom Journal***, remember to take deep relaxing breaths and count your blessings!

. . . .

You have a wealth of team members assisting you to plan your wedding, yes? And gratitude is a big part of teamwork. At each fitting for your gown or meeting with your wedding coordinator or design session with your florist, let "your team" know how much they are appreciated. An extra "thank you" to someone is like a lucky coin: it just keeps creating abundant blessings.

~ A SIXPENCE FOR YOUR SHOE ~

No. 2: A Silver Token

The use of the acclaimed sixpence began in the British Empire in 1551, and the coin was last issued in 1967. The early sixpence coins were made of silver, a metal known as "a natural antibiotic used to purify food and water for thousands of years," according to shoe historian Cameron Kippen. "Therefore the significance of the silver coin in the ancient bridal tradition may have been to wish the bride good *health* as well as *wealth* and prosperity in her forthcoming union."

Building on the legend of silver, metaphorically, it is said to "mirror the soul." So perhaps putting the silver coin in the bride's shoe was a way to bestow a wealth of *spiritual blessings* on her marriage as well. New coins may no longer be silver, but the blessings they represent are just as abundant.

The sixpence, in the form of currency, was around for over four hundred years yet still has sentimental value today as a token of abundance and good wishes. To ensure that your *love* has that kind of longevity, what do you need to declare about your commitment, change in your relationship, or promise your heart? Abundance is infinite; so think big, broad, deep—it's all possible!

~A SIXPENCE FOR YOUR SHOE~

No. 3: A Grateful Heart

Do you think that abundance is limited? That good fortune skips a day in your life? Wise spiritual guides tell us that what we might consider as lack of abundance or misfortune is an opportunity to open our hearts even wider, a reminder to be thankful for what we do have. Blessings *come a'calling* to a grateful heart!

The Roman philosopher Cicero said over two thousand years ago that *"a grateful heart is the greatest virtue."* We receive presents each day that we may not recognize as presents, but it seems that anytime we express appreciation for the experience we've been given—no matter what it is—then our hearts open that much more. Keep your heart available for love in abundant proportions…and abundance is yours. Remember that it's a generous dose of gratitude that returns you to the "fortunes" of love.

. . . .

There simply cannot be too many thank-yous spoken in the world. (Nor too many hearts full of love!) Keep the gratitude going. Say "thank you" to the first and last person you see today—and everyone in between. Make it your job to light people up. It feels great; in fact, you're the one that just might get the biggest reward. Love is abundantly endless…you won't run out!

~ A SIXPENCE FOR YOUR SHOE ~

No. 4: Love Pats Left and Right

I've read that originally the custom was to place a coin in the bride's *left* shoe. Early cultures, tuned in to the subtle energies of the body, knew that the left side of the body connects to the right side of the brain that links to one's intuitive and creative abilities. So did they surmise that this "left-shoe custom" became more of a guarantee for prosperity or even spiritual guidance? Or was it because, historically, the left side of the body is considered the "female" side, therefore putting the coin in the left shoe helped ensure motherhood and blessings for a healthy family?

Whew! Maybe it's just easier if we don't try to figure out some of those ancient customs. Whatever the superstition (or scientific connection) in the past, on *your* wedding day if there is no comfortable spot in "either" shoe to tuck your sixpence or penny, perhaps tuck it into the hem of your dress or in your bodice—on the *left* side just in case! Or slip the coin in *his* left pocket as you meet him at the altar. Wherever it goes, give it a little *love pat* to extend its abundance a million fold.

Give *yourself* a little love pat right now—on your left shoulder, then your right shoulder for balance. Being your own best friend is an *abundant* gift indeed; as the wise Abraham Lincoln advised, "Retain the friend within." Listen to your intuition, use your creativity and give yourself what feeds your feminine spirit, your love energy, and your generous heart. Now, go share those love pats—left and right!

~A SIXPENCE FOR YOUR SHOE~

No. 5: Declare Your Own Value

In the old-world custom of a woman's dowry (the wealth she brought to the marriage from her family) lies the tradition of the bridal sixpence coin. Silver or gold coins would have been included in the bride's dowry along with livestock, land, and household goods. Therefore, putting a coin into the bride's shoe—originally done by her father in most areas of the world—symbolized transferring this wealth to the groom to ensure a prosperous life for his new family.

What symbolizes a "rich" life to you? What do you bring to your relationship that offers an abundant spirit? Is part of your "dowry" a generous helping of lightheartedness?

. . . .

History can be rather convoluted and, at times, not very attractive. Today, a man and woman's sense of "wealth" includes riches of the heart and spirit—generating an abundant partnership and deep connection. We are blessed in modern culture to be able to declare our own value. *You* are an invaluable part of the divine plan—wear it well!

~A SIXPENCE FOR YOUR SHOE~

No. 6: Wedding Slippers

Our fascination with shoes started long before designer labels or "Sex and the City." Shoes—for obvious reasons—were first created for protective covering but then evolved into status symbols (sometimes rather foreboding ones) as well as objects of beauty and sexual allure.

Historians tell us that the symbolism of footwear in connection with marriage and luck dates back to antiquity. An old custom in China, tossing the bride's red shoes from a roof, ensured the couple's happiness; the ancient Inca Indians of Peru exchanged sandals to seal the marriage deal.

In many old-world countries, shoes became a harsh symbol of man's authority over women. But more gentle footwear stories emerge in bridal history: the old custom of a Zuni bride's fiancé lovingly handcrafting leather wedding boots for her; or generations of mothers, skilled at needlework, ornately embroidering their daughter's delicate silk wedding slippers; or the Cinderella-like tradition from Northern Italy where all the wedding guests tried on the bride's shoe.

With so much attention on shoes and their intriguing history—no matter the style of this prized icon—it stands to reason that the symbol for wealth, a coin, was placed in the bride's shoe.

· ·

There are many times in history when it may have been hard for a woman to hold on to her sense of self-worth. But just imagine the first bride so confident that on her wedding day, she placed a silver coin in her shoe herself and felt she was standing in her own power and purpose!

Look deep into *your* true desire and find your strength. Trust *your* spirit and find your purpose. Open up *your* heart and find your love. Then on your wedding day, you don't have to "do" anything to express your authentic spirit, you'll just "be" what you've found.

~ A SIXPENCE FOR YOUR SHOE ~

$\mathcal{N}$o. 7: *Memory of Love*

One of my favorite quotations, "Gratitude is the memory of the heart," reminds me to look deeper into my own heart in case I've missed acknowledging someone for a contribution to my life. Nestled there, I always find a memory of love.

Weddings are a busy time where you're creating loads of memories—surrounded by more people than ever making a contribution to you. Some contributions you are aware of while others remain a mystery. How do you keep up and thank everyone?

That's why I like the old bridal custom of carrying a coin (whether it's a sixpence, penny, franc, florin, or dime!) because it's a great reminder of your true wealth—your love. And love is always followed by gratitude...and gratitude just naturally flows out from a full heart...and a full heart has perfect memory. No one gets left out when under love's influence.

Have you missed acknowledging someone during the flurry of wedding planning? Perhaps it's *you*—give yourself a rousing *"that a girl"* right now! You have accomplished wonders planning a beautiful wedding where people will carry home a piece of your love in their hearts...a lasting memory. *That a girl!*

~A SIXPENCE FOR YOUR SHOE~

No. 8: A Wealth of Fertile Wishes

Flowers, cakes, and children used as a part of wedding festivities were all originally symbolic of the desire for "fertility." Many ancient customs came from the wish of the community for the couple to be blessed with children as well as an abundant and full life. Times have changed through the centuries, but a community's "fertile" wishes of well-being and happiness remain universal.

How does your community express tradition? Even if your community's ways are not how you do things now, there is still a way to include what's at the heart of the matter—their love. And whether or not you use any rituals or traditions for your wedding (putting a coin in your shoe or purse, cutting a big wedding cake, having a flower girl, or tossing a bouquet) you will be just as married, just as capable to live an abundant life, and just as able to find ways to include your community's well-wishes of love!

Modern weddings may use many decorative elements just because we find them beautiful, fashionable, eco-friendly, or traditional. Whatever the reason behind your decisions for your wedding, add your own sense of abundance and spirit, having the choices express *your* essence! This way you bring energy of the present moment into each choice. What could be more "fertile"...more beautiful?

~ A SIXPENCE FOR YOUR SHOE ~

No. 9: *The Prickly Beloved*

Before the fabled sixpence existed in the British Empire, coins minted in Scotland used the image of their national flower, the beloved thistle, as a symbol of honor. Then later the thistle joined other botanical images—roses, leeks, and shamrocks—in a garland on the back of the sixpence coin itself.

I wouldn't consider the picturesque thistle a romantic wildflower—full of prickly leaves and bristly stems. Author Laura Martin concurs in *Wildflower Folklore*: "Since the language of this plant is defiance and surliness, a young lady would probably not be pleased to see thistle in her bouquet from an admirer."

However, beloved it is and a perfect *aide memoire*...a reminder right there on the back of your sixpence coin that it's great to have people around who love us even on our "prickly" days!

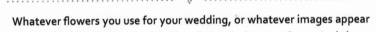

Whatever flowers you use for your wedding, or whatever images appear on your bridal coin, be thankful for all the choices you have. And those times when you're feeling a bit thistle-like (pretty to look at, but a tad prickly), at least blow loving "long-distant" kisses to your fans and let everyone know you'll soon be back in full bloom!

~A SIXPENCE FOR YOUR SHOE~

No. 10: *Untie the Ribbons*

Yes, I know you keep up with the details of the wedding presents you've been given, but how about the "gifts of the universe" you receive every day? Take a minute to jot down in your ***Wisdom Journal*** notes about these gifts that may go unnoticed as gifts: a beautiful sunset, a rainy day, a nourishing breakfast, a happy greeting from your postman. And in the moment of recognizing and appreciating them, you realize how rich you really are.

Every day is a blessed day! Every day is an opportunity to celebrate *simple gifts.* Like the eighteenth century Shaker hymn reminds us: *'Tis the gift to be simple, 'tis the gift to be free, 'tis the gift to come down where we ought to be; and when we find ourselves in the place just right, 'twill be in the valley of love and delight.*

Celebrate your abundance of love and delight!

Let your vintage sixpence, wedding penny, or lucky dime represent the blessings of simple gifts all around you. *"Each day comes bearing its own gifts. Untie the ribbons,"* Ruth Ann Schabacker prompts us. Keep your heart open so the riches of life have a place to land!

PART II

$\mathscr{W}$OMEN'S WISDOM

1. YOU AND THE WOMEN AROUND YOU

*P*art of the joys of a bride's rite-of-passage is to be able to connect with her heritage of being a woman. Whatever your relationship with the women in your world—family, friends, work associates—now is the time to open your heart, clean up old wounds, request support, and allow their contributions in. Invite their womanly wisdom into your world.

- What if planning your wedding became a practice for building a community of love and support for the rest of your life?

- What if your time as a bride taught you to "receive" as graciously as you "gave"? (Or vice versa.)

- What if you were completely open for your attendants to "attend" to your emotional and spiritual well-being as well as assist with wedding activities? (What would you have to adjust to allow yourself to be lovingly nurtured by your friends and family?)

- What if you allowed yourself to feel beautiful and loved every day?

- What if you asked for exactly what your heart desired?

- What if planning a wedding introduced you to a dazzling and perhaps unknown womanly heritage?

- What if "thank you" began every conversation you had?

- What if how you planned your wedding was how you did everything? (Is there a life lesson there?)

- What if the experience of planning your wedding was practice for growing into the woman you want to become?

- What if your interactions with your attendants, mother, step-mother, future mother-in-law, or (fill in the blank) were an exercise in forgiveness?

As you use *The Bride's Ritual Guide*—reading the collection of *RitualWise* **Bridal Notes** and the "wise-woman" quotes in the *Wisdom Journal*—wrap yourself in your womanly heritage. Allow any insights to contribute to your self-discovery and invite the women in your life to participate with you on your journey!

2. HOW TO USE YOUR *WISDOM JOURNAL*

*E*ach page of the **Wisdom Journal** has a little "something borrowed"—wise words "borrowed" from women around the world—with space to add *your* own bits of wisdom. Keep this book with you so you can turn to the **Wisdom Journal** section and jot down inspirations and insights, including those that come up when reading the *RitualWise* **Bridal Notes**. Add favorite quotations and poems; enter your dream remembrances; record ideas for creating a life you love and whatever pours from your heart during your bridal rite-of-passage.

The purpose of the **Wisdom Journal** is to deepen your bridal experience by encouraging you to write down all the "love notes" of your spirit. When you put your vision and intentions on paper, you give them "come true" power! What does your heart say today? Record it in your **Wisdom Journal**…and be prepared for a bit of magic.

Wisdom Journal ℘

...only love is real.
~ Marianne Williamson

We can only learn to love by loving.
~ Iris Murdoch

Until you make peace with who you are,
you'll never be content with what you have.
~ Doris Mortman

All you need to do to receive guidance
is to ask for it and then listen.
~ Sanaya Roman

*A woman is the full circle. Within her is the
power to create, nurture, and transform.*

~ Diane Mariechild

*Surround yourself with people who
respect and treat you well.*
~ Claudia Black

The future is made of the same stuff as the present.
~ Simone Weil

We are the hero of our own story.
~ Mary McCarthy

*Learn to get in touch with the silence within yourself
and know that everything in this life has a purpose.*
~ Elisabeth Kübler-Ross

Nobody ever measured, even poets,
how much the heart can hold.
~ Zelda Fitzgerald

Listening is a form of accepting.

~ Stella Terrill Mann

The giving of love is an education in itself.

~ Eleanor Roosevelt

Gratitude is what returns us to Love.
~ Lisa Clapier

Love is, or it ain't. Thin love ain't love at all.
~ Toni Morrison

In real love you want the other person's good.
In romantic love you want the other person.

~ Margaret Anderson

Trust in yourself. Your perceptions are often far more accurate than you are willing to believe.

~ Claudia Black

*You need to claim the events of your life
to make yourself yours.*
~ Anne Wilson Schaef

*To love deeply in one direction
makes us more loving in all others.*
~ Anne-Sophie Swetchine

We need to be willing to let our intuition guide us, and then be willing to follow that guidance directly and fearlessly.

~ Shakti Gawain

*Love is the difficult realization that
something other than oneself is real.*
~ Iris Murdoch

Saying no can be the ultimate self-care.

~ Claudia Black

Life shrinks or expands in proportion to one's courage.

~ Anais Nin

If you judge people, you have no time to love them.
~ Mother Teresa

To love is to receive a glimpse of heaven.
~ Karen Sunde

Listening keeps my heart unclenched.
Listening is active openness.

~ Danielle LaPorte

_____

_____

_____

_____

_____

_____

_____

_____

_____

_____

_____

_____

_____

_____

_____

_____

_____

_____

_____

I've looked at love from both sides now /
From give and take, and still somehow /
It's love's illusions I recall /
I really don't know love at all.

~ Joni Mitchell

*Love doesn't just sit there, like a stone, it has to be made,
like bread; re-made all the time, made new.*

~ Ursula K. Le Guinn

The important thing is not to think much but to love much;
do, then whatever most arouses you to love.
~ Saint Teresa of Avila

You must love and care for yourself,
because that's when the best comes out.

~ Tina Turner

Love is what we were born with.
Fear is what we learned here.
~ Marianne Williamson

If we really want to love, we must learn how to forgive.

~ Mother Teresa

Where your attention goes, so goes your life.
~ Cynthia Zaal

Listen to your heart above all voices.

~ Marta Kagan

Look inside to find yourself.
~ Cornelia Powell

POSTSCRIPT

*W*oman-to-Woman

"Something Borrowed" Ritual Exchange:
Share Your Bridal Experience

I invite you to participate in the Woman-to-Woman "Something Borrowed" Ritual Exchange.

- Do you have a story about how you, friends, or family members used the *"something old, something new, something borrowed, something blue, and a sixpence for your shoe"* rhyme for your/their wedding?

- Do you know of resources for items for brides to use for the rhyme?

Email them to info@WeddingsOfGrace.com and chosen ones will be posted in my *Weddings of Grace* Online Magazine (www.Weddings OfGrace.com) for other brides to "borrow" and enjoy! I look forward to hearing from you and reading your stories, ideas and bits of wisdom.

Thank you!

CP

PRODUCTS AND RESOURCES

Ideas from the *RitualWise* Bridal Notes

~Breathing and Relaxing Exercises:

BOOKS

* *Free Your Breath, Free Your Life* by Dennis Lewis

* *Breathe Into Being: Awakening to Who You Really Are* by Dennis Lewis

* *The Breathing Book: Vitality & Good Health Through Essential Breath Work* by Donna Farhi

  See these and other selections at www.WeddingsOfGrace.com, then click on Art of Being a Woman Bookstore and scroll down to "Meditation & Breath."

CDs

* *Open Your Heart* Meditation CD for Brides: This is my guided meditation CD (and there is one for all Women as well). See www.WeddingsOfGrace.com and click on "Products."

* Kathy Freston's Transformational Meditation Series: See www.WeddingsOfGrace.com, then click on Especially for Brides Bookstore and scroll down to "Meditation CDs."

~Lavender essential oil:

Mountain Rose Herbs: See www.WeddingsOfGrace.com, click on "Products" and scroll down to the Mountain Rose Herbs section.

~Relaxing Music:

- *The Yearning: Romances for Alto Flute* by Michael Hoppe & Tim Wheater

- *At Ease* by Dharma Moon

- *Hidden Waters/Sacred Ground* by Sophia

   See my online bookstore for these and other soothing suggestions. Go to www.WeddingsOfGrace.com, click on Especially for Brides Bookstore and scroll down to "Music."

~Ribbons for Bookmarks (to mark your ***RitualWise* Bridal Notes** and ***Wisdom Journal*** pages and for making "True-Love Knots"):

- Gloriana Threads: A beautiful selection of hand-dyed silk ribbons. See their website for a list of retailers. www.GlorianaThreads.com

- Midori Ribbons: One of my favorite ribbon sources for a variety of styles, including a pretty metallic ribbon. Check their website to find a retailer near you: www.MidoriRibbon.com

~Vintage Sixpence:

I've made it easy for you to get your very own vintage sixpence through *Weddings of Grace* Online Magazine, packaged in a sweet little gift bag with a copy of the famous bridal rhyme. See www.WeddingsOfGrace.com and click on "Products" and scroll down to Vintage Sixpence.

~Vintage Handkerchiefs:

Lois Lamb: Lois was one of the first antique linen dealers I met when I had my shop in Atlanta during the 1980s and 90s. And she still sells beautifully restored vintage handkerchiefs, perfect to use for your wedding. www.VintageLinens.com.

SPECIAL NOTE:

My FREE e-Book, *Tips for a Sensuous Bride: 39 Calming & Naturally Fragrant Ways to Be the Bride You Want to Be*, is full of calming ideas and products. Get it for FREE to download when you register at my online magazine, *Weddings of Grace*, www.WeddingsOfGrace.com, or my blogs, *Letters to a Bride*, www.CorneliaPowellWeddings.blogspot.com, or *The Woman You Become*, www.WomanYouBecome.com.

ACKNOWLEDGMENTS

*T*hank you to each of the thousands of brides I worked with over the years—including all the mothers, fathers, fiancés and friends who loved them. Thank you all for sharing your lives, various rites-of-passages, stories, concerns, dreams, humor, and passions with me.

Thank you to the women and men who shared their bits of wisdom, research and insights for this book. Thank you to the photographers who provided their beautiful photographs to highlight a bride's rite-of-passage. (See their names and contact information on a following page.)

Thank you. I love you all.

PHOTOGRAPH CREDITS

I thank these wonderful artists for sharing their beautiful photographs with *The Bride's Ritual Guide*:

Paige Christie: Bryson City, North Carolina
www.PLCPhoto.com

Beth Ely for Missy McLamb Photographers: Pittsboro, North Carolina & New York, New York
www.MissyMcLamb.com

Julie Mikos: Berkeley, California
www.JulieMikos.com

Priscilla Wannamaker: Atlanta, Georgia
www.PWannamaker.com

BIBLIOGRAPHY

Anderson, Emily Elizabeth. *Eco-Chic Weddings: Simple Tips to Plan an Environmentally Friendly, Socially Responsible, Affordable, and Stylish Celebration.* New York: Hatherleigh Press, 2007.

Azar-Rucquoi, Adele. *Money as Sacrament: Finding the Sacred in Money (A Book for Women).* Berkeley: Celestial Arts, 2002.

Baldizzone, Tiziana and Gianni. *Wedding Ceremonies: Ethnic Symbols, Costume and Rituals.* Italy: Flammarion, 2001.

Barton, Leslie and Sherri Leigh Myers. *The Bride Revealed: An Intimate Look Behind the Wedding Veil.* Kansas City: Andrews McMeel Publishing, 2005.

Bata Shoe Museum. *All About Shoes: Footwear Through the Ages.* Canada: Bata Shoe Organization, 1994.

Cohen, David. "Marriage and Adulthood," *The Circle of Life: Rituals from the Human Family Album.* New York: Harper Collins Publishers, 1991.

Foster, Helen Bradley and Donald Clay Johnson, editors. *Wedding Dress Across Cultures.* Oxford: Berg Publishers, 2003.

Gilbert, Elizabeth. *Eat, Pray, Love: One Woman's Search for Everything Across Italy, India, and Indonesia*. New York: Penguin Books, 2006.

Gilman, Susan Jane. *Hypocrite in a Pouffy White Dress: Tales of Growing Up Groovy and Clueless*. New York: Warner Books, 2005.

Howard, Vicki. *Brides, Inc. American Weddings and the Business of Tradition*. Pennsylvania: University of Pennsylvania Press, 2006.

Jones, Kathy. *The Ancient British Goddess: Her Myths, Legends, Sacred Sites, and Present Day Revelation*. Somerset, England: Green Magic, 2002.

Kippen, Cameron. "Foottalk," http://foottalk.blogspot.com/2006/02/something-old-something-new.html.

Lewis, Dennis. *Free Your Breath, Free Your Life: How Conscious Breathing Can Relieve Stress, Increase Vitality, and Help You Live More Fully*. Boston: Shambhala, 2004.

Martin, Laura C. *Wildflower Folklore*. Charlotte, North Carolina: The East Woods Press, 1984.

Monsarrat, Ann. *And the Bride Wore... The Story of the White Wedding*. London: Gentry Books, 1973.

Plonka, Lavinia. *What Are You Afraid Of?: A Body/Mind Guide to Courageous Living*, New York: Penguin Group, 2005.

Powell, Cornelia. "I Will Tell Thee A Supreme Mystery" and "Simple Gifts," *Weddings of Grace*, www.WeddingsOfGrace.com.

Seebo, Donna. www.DelphiInternational.com

Tober, Barbara. *The Bride: A Celebration*. New York: Harry N. Abrams, Inc., 1984.

Wallace, Carol McD. *All Dressed in White: The Irresistible Rise of the American Wedding*. New York: Penguin Books, 2004.

Walsch, Neale Donald. "I Believe God Wants You to Know," www. NealeDonaldWalsch.com.

Williamson, Marianne. *A Return to Love: Reflections of the Principles of A Course in Miracles*. New York: HarperCollins Publishers, 1992.

Winn, Michael. *Way of the Inner Smile*, www.HealingTaoUsa.com.

INDEX

A

All Dressed in White (Wallace)   xvi, 3, 59

The Ancient British Goddess (Jones) 68

And the Bride Wore... The Story of the White Wedding (Monsarrat)   5

Anderson, Emily Elizabeth 56
    Eco-chic Weddings

Anderson, Margaret   116

Ayurvedic   71

Azar-Rucquoi, Adele   60
    Money as Sacrament

B

Bailey, Philip James 45

Baldizzone, Tiziana and Gianni 5
    Wedding Ceremonies: Ethnic Symbols, Costume and Rituals

Barton, Leslie   28
    The Bride Revealed

Black, Claudia   107, 117, 122

breath/s   xxi, xxii, 17-18, 26, 33, 39, 41–42, 44–47, 55, 70, 72, 74, 81

Breathe Into Being (Lewis) 139

The Breathing Book (Farhi) 139

bridal veil (see veil)

The Bride: A Celebration (Tober)   3

The Bride Revealed (Barton) 30

Bride's magazine 3, 32

Brigit (Celtic goddess)   68

Brockway, Rev. Laurie Sue vi
    The Wedding Goddess

C

The Canterbury Tales (Chaucer) 4

Celtic Blessings 57

ceremony   xv–xvi, 8, 17, 27-28, 43, 70

Charles, Prince 69

Chaucer, Geoffrey 4
    The Canterbury Tales

Cherokee Wedding Prayer 57

Christie, Paige 8, 145

Cicero 83

Clapier, Lisa 114

Coleridge, Hartley 39

Conversations with God (Walsch)   40

D

dowry 85
Dr. DooLady (aka Dr. Kathlyn) 73

E

Eat, Pray, Love (Gilbert) 41
Eco-chic Weddings (Anderson) 56
eco-friendly 56, 88
Elizabeth, Princess 59
Ely, Beth 23, 65, 145
eyes of love 39

F

Farhi, Donna 139
     The Breathing Book
Fashion Research Centre (Bath,
     England) 6
favours 67
Fitzgerald, Zelda 111
forget-me-nots 76
Free Your Breath, Free Your Life
     (Lewis) 139
Freston, Kathy 139

G

Gawain, Shakti 120
Gilbert, Elizabeth 41
     Eat, Pray, Love
Gilman, Susan Jane 25
     Hypocrite in a Pouffy
     White Dress
goddess 12, 34, 48, 60, 68
Gloriana Threads 140

H

handkerchief/hankie 7, 26–27
Hoffman, Phyllis vi
Hypocrite in a Pouffy White Dress
     (Gilman) 25

J

Jeaffreson, John Cordy 6
Johnson, Luci Baines 6
Jones, Kathy 68
     The Ancient British Goddess

K

Kagan, Marta 134
Kueller, Anik vii
Kippen, Cameron 4-5, 82
Kübler-Ross, Elisabeth 113

L

Lamb, Lois 141
LaPorte, Danielle vi, 126
lavender 26, 72, 140
law of attraction 8
Le Guinn, Ursula K. 128
Letters to a Bride xix, 141
Lewis, Dennis 46, 139
     Breathe Into Being
     Free Your Breath, Free
     Your Life
Lincoln, Abraham 84

M

Mann, Stella Terrill 112
Mariechild, Diane 106
Martin, Laura 89
    Wildflower Folklore
Mary, mother of Jesus (Virgin
    Mary) 4, 68
McCarthy, Mary 109
McLamb, Missy 23, 65, 145
meditation 16, 74, 139
Meiland-Shaw, Lara vii
Midori Ribbons 140
Mikos, Julie xvi, xxii, 96, 145
Mitchell, Joni 127
Money as Sacrament
    (Azar-Rucquoi) 60
Monsarrat, Ann 5, 8, 67
    And the Bride Wore…The Story
    of the White Wedding
Morrison, Toni 115
Mortman, Doris 104
Mother Teresa 124, 132
Mountain Rose Herbs 140
Murdoch, Iris 103, 121
Museum of Costume 6

N

Nin, Anais 123
Nolan, Maureen vii

O

Open Your Heart Meditations for
    Brides 16, 139
orange blossom 29, 33

P

penny 81, 84, 87, 90
Plonka, Lavinia 46
Popular Antiquities 6

Q

Queen Victoria 34, 69

R

rite-of-passage xv–xvi, xix, xxi–xxii,
    8, 11–12, 30, 40, 44, 61, 71, 74,
    95, 99, 143
Roman, Sanaya 105
Roosevelt, Eleanor 113

S

sapphire 69, 74
Schabacker, Ruth Ann 90
Schaef, Anne Wilson 118
Scotland 5, 89
Shaker hymn 90
Shakespeare, William 57, 68
shoe/s xxii, 4, 6, 11–12, 16, 79–90,
    137
silver 4, 6, 82, 85
silver coin
    See silver

sixpence xxii, 4–6, 11–12, 16, 79–90,
        137
sixpence for your shoe
        See sixpence
smile 47, 73
Smith, Jeanne Dudley vi
something blue xxii, 4–7, 11–12,
        16, 65–76, 137
something borrowed xxii, 4–6, 11,
        16, 51–62, 137
something new xxii, 4–7, 11, 16,
        37–48, 137
something old xxii, 4–7, 11, 16,
        23–34, 137
Spencer, Lady Diana 69
Sunde, Karen 125
Swetchine, Anne-Sophie 119

T

Teresa of Avila, Saint 129
thistle 89
Tips for a Sensuous Bride (Powell)
        141
Tober, Barbara 3, 32
        The Bride: A Celebration
true blue 75
true-love knot 67
Turner, Tina 130

V

veil 6, 7, 29–30
Victoria magazine vi
Victorian 5, 26, 67

W

Wallace, Carol McD. xvi, 3, 25, 59
        All Dressed in White
Walsch, Neale Donald 40
        Conversations with God
Wannamaker, Priscilla 1, 37, 51, 79,
        93, 145
*Wedding Ceremonies: Ethnic
        Symbols, Costume and Rituals*
        (Baldizzone) 5
wedding coin 81
wedding dress/wedding gown vii,
        7, 25, 31–32, 34, 43, 54, 59–60,
        67
wedding handkerchief/hankie
        See handkerchief/hankie
The Wedding Goddess (Brockway) vi
wedding slippers 86
wedding veil
        See veil
Weddings of Grace xvi, xix, 16, 137,
        139–141
Weil, Simone 108
Wildflower Folklore (Martin) 89
Williamson, Marianne 102, 131
The Woman You Become 141

Z

Zaal, Cynthia 133

Made in the USA
Charleston, SC
02 May 2014